Fish for Dinner

Story by Dawn McMillan
Illustrations by Jenny Mountstephen

Harcourt Achieve

Rigby • Saxon • Steck-Vaughn

www.HarcourtAchieve.com
1.800.531.5015

PM Extensions

Emerald

U.S. Edition © 2013 HMH Supplemental Publishers
10801 N. MoPac Expressway
Building #3
Austin, TX 78759
www.hmhsupplemental.com

Text © 2005 Cengage Learning Australia Pty Limited
Illustrations © 2005 Cengage Learning Australia Pty Limited
Originally published in Australia by Cengage Learning Australia

11   1957   17
24548

Text: Dawn McMillan
Illustrations: Jenny Mountstephen
Reprint: Siew Han Ong
Printed in China by 1010 Printing International Ltd

Fish for Dinner
ISBN 978 0 75 789363 6

Contents

CHAPTER **1**

Along the Coast

The road to our favorite fishing place twists and turns along the coast. It's narrow and in some places there's barely enough room for the cars to pass.

Nikki and I love going along that road. From one side of the car we can see tall banks with big trees bending over us. From the other side we can see the sea.

Sometimes the sea is still, lying quietly against the rocks. Sometimes it crashes and splashes high in the air.

Mom never takes us fishing when the sea is rough. "There'll be no fish," she says. "They won't come close in when the sea is too choppy."

Actually she's thinking of us, not the fish. She's keeping us safe. She always tells us not to take risks with the sea.

The best time for fishing along the coast is when the tide is just starting to come in. When the water is low, there are lots of places where we can push our rod holders deep into the sand.

At our favorite beach we can swim as well as fish.

Mom teases us and says, "All that splashing will scare the fish away!"

We have to keep moving the rod holders up the beach as the water comes in, and we have to move our picnic blanket and towels, too.

I remember one time when the water tricked us and a wave washed over my towel. Mom and Nikki laughed and laughed.

From our beach we can see people fishing way out on the rocks, casting their lines into the deeper water. Sometimes, when I see the rods bending, I want to go there, too.

Mom says we're much safer here though. The rocks can be slippery, and out there you can get caught by the tide.

What happened today proves she is right!

CHAPTER 2

Stopping the Traffic

When I woke up this morning, the sun was shining. No wind, I thought.

I woke Nikki and we raced downstairs to Mom's room. "Come on, Mom!" we shouted. "It's a perfect day for fishing!"

Mom sat up and looked out the window. "You're right," she said. "No sleeping in for me this morning, not with such eager fishers in the family!"

While Mom cooked breakfast and made our picnic lunch, Nikki and I put the fishing gear in the car. I remembered to put all the bait into a plastic container. Mom didn't like the smell of bait in the car. By ten o'clock we were on the road.

When we arrived at the beach, the tide was way out. We had plenty of time to set up our picnic spot before the tide turned. Then we were ready to catch some fish.

But all day the lines were still.

"The only bites we're getting are ours!" Nikki laughed, as she munched on her sandwich.

Then just before 2 o'clock the wind came up. The sea turned choppy, and it was time to go home. That's when our real adventure began!

We'd just started our drive home along the coast road when suddenly we saw a dog, sitting right in the middle of the road!

"Mom! Stop!" screamed Nikki.

"Someone must've hit him!" I shouted, as Mom pulled the car to the side of the road and switched the hazard lights on.

CHAPTER 3

Emergency!

I started to push my door open when Mom yelled at me. "No, Ben! Get out on the bank side and stay there. I'll see what's wrong!"

"Be careful, Mom." I heard Nikki whisper.

As Mom got out of the car, the dog stood up and barked.

"There's nothing wrong with him," I said to Nikki. "Quick, Mom!" I shouted. "Get him off the road!"

Back at the car Mom said, "He seems OK, but he's very upset."

I looked at the dog's collar. "She's a girl and her name's Lucy," I said.

"She wants to cross the road – back to the sea!" Nikki shouted. "She's worried!"

Nikki was right. Lucy was pulling away, wanting us to follow.

"Come on then, Lucy," Mom sighed. "Onward we go! Nikki! Ben! You stay on this side of me. Can't be too careful on this road."

Lucy led us along the road, and then down the bank to the sea. As we scrambled down, we heard someone calling, "Help me, please!"

Lucy leaped away from Mom and down over the rocks.

"There's a man down there, Mom!" Nikki shouted, pointing out to where the waves were breaking. "Look! Over there! He's lying on that big flat rock!"

"He's hurt!" I cried, as I started to climb down the rocks.

"Wait!" shouted Mom. "It's too dangerous. We'll go and get the car. If we bring it closer and park on this side of the road, it will be easier to get the things we need. We can reach him from that little beach over there."

"Yes," said Nikki. "We'll take him a blanket to keep him warm."

"I'll put my jacket here, Mom," I said. "On the side of the road. Then when we bring the car back we'll know just where he is."

"That's a great idea," said Mom proudly.

Then we all called down to the man.

"We're coming!" we shouted. "We'll get help! Stay there, Lucy!"

CHAPTER 4

Getting Help

We took the car to a safe turning place and came back to park, just past my jacket and near the little beach.

"We'll need the first aid kit," said Mom. "And that blanket, Nikki."

"And your phone, Mom!" I remembered. "We might need to call an ambulance."

As we hurried along the beach, Lucy came bounding to meet us, still barking loudly.

"It's all right, girl," I said as I bent to pat her. "We're here to help now."

Lucy turned and led us along sandy tracks, out to the rocks where the man lay still. He was shivering, and looked very pale.

"I slipped – I think I've broken my leg," he whispered. "I thought I could get back, but . . . " His voice faded away, and he grimaced in pain.

Mom turned to us and said quietly, "We need to move fast. The tide is coming in."

Then she knelt down beside the fisherman to find out his name and reassure him. "Don't worry," she said. "We'll look after you!"

"I'm glad you brought the blanket, Nikki," said Mom. "Stefan's in shock and needs to be kept warm."

"I'll call the ambulance, Mom. I know how to do it," I said.

"Good," said Mom. "Just make sure they know where to come."

"They can't miss us!" I smiled. "The car will show them where to stop."

Mom and Nikki sat with Stefan while I called the emergency services.

When the operator answered, I said, "We need an ambulance, please, to Southern Coast Road, about half way between Seahaven and Grahamstown. There's a fisherman hurt on the rocks. You'll see a red car parked on the seaside of the road. The hazard lights on the car are on."

I gave the operator my name and our phone number, and she seemed very pleased with all my information. Then I remembered to tell her about the tide.

"Don't worry, Ben," she said. "The ambulance will be there in plenty of time."

CHAPTER 5

The Rescue

I put the phone in my pocket and went back to join the others. As I sat down, Lucy licked my face. "It's okay, girl," I said, rubbing her neck. "We're looking after your friend."

Mom smiled and said, "Stefan, this is Ben. He's just called the rescue squad for you."

Stefan turned his face to look at me. "Thanks!" he said.

It seemed to take hours for the ambulance to come. Mom, Nikki, and I sat quietly and watched the water come closer. Lucy curled up close against Stefan's chest.

"Look, Ben," said Nikki. "Lucy knows to keep Stefan warm."

Finally we heard the sirens. We leaped to our feet and looked back along the road. We could see flashing lights coming nearer and nearer. Suddenly the ambulance came around the bend and pulled to a stop, just in front of our car. A red rescue vehicle followed close behind. "They're here, Stefan!" I shouted, and he sighed and closed his eyes.

Nikki and Mom waved. "Over here!" they called. "He's over here!"

The paramedics made their way to where Stefan was lying. The water was higher now, so there was less beach for them to walk on. They climbed easily over the rocks, carrying their equipment and a stretcher.

"I'm so glad you're here!" Mom said. "We think his leg is broken. We just wanted to keep him still and warm, but the tide is worrying us."

The paramedics looked at Stefan's leg. "Mmm. Broken all right!" one said. "We'll have you to the hospital in no time, and you'll probably be home again tomorrow."

"No rock fishing for a while," the other joked. "You'll just have to settle for buying fish."

CHAPTER 6

The Catch of the Day

And that should have been the end of the story – Stefan safely rescued, and Nikki, Mom, and I starting to head for home with Lucy. But no!

In all the time we were with Stefan, no one had thought about his fishing gear. We were too busy looking after him to pay any attention to his two rods jammed into the rocks, or to the open fishing box nearby.

Then, just as the paramedic joked about buying fish, I looked up. The rod closer to us was bent over, the line straight and tight in the water.

"Look! He's got one!" I shouted. "Stefan won't have to get his fish from the store after all!"

I jumped up to pull the fish in.

"Wait!" called Mom. "I'll help you. It's slippery out there!"

So Mom and I pulled in the fish while Nikki cheered.

"It's a big one, Stefan!" she yelled to him. "Just wait till you see it!"

As Stefan was carried away on a stretcher, Nikki and I held up the fish for him.

"It's the best fish I've ever caught there!" he said, trying to smile. "I think you should have it. I don't think I'll be able to cook it tonight . . . "

"No," Mom agreed. "But we could cook it for you tomorrow night when we bring Lucy back."

"Yes!" I said. "And we could bring some steak for Lucy. She risked her life to stop the traffic and get help."

As they were ready to shut the ambulance door, Stefan smiled weakly. "Thank you for looking after me," he whispered. "I'll see you tomorrow, and we'll share the fish."

"But not the steak," laughed Nikki. "Lucy can have the steak all to herself. She saved your life. She's your hero!"